Praises for

Raising Today's

Sipping on a hot beverage while listening to a wise mind giving sobering counsel on parenting is what this book offers you. It was quite refreshing how relatable the author was in her book as if having a one-on-one conversation with the reader. In this book are practical counsels fit for every mom and dad who need guidance and encouragement on how to manoeuvre the challenges of parenting a teen for now and eternity. Enjoy the practical but profound advice given in this book and use its counsel to invest in a healthy future for your parent-teen relationship.

SANIA AND DR COURTNEY DOOKIE

Directors of Dookie Institute

Fort McMurray, Alberta, Canada

What an amazing and insightful piece of work! The author did a great job sharing her experience, providing guidance, and also relating parenting to scripture. I believe this piece of work will be of great value to most parents.

LOLA ABHULIMEN

Philadelphia, USA

Raising Today's Teens is packed with powerful truths, thought-provoking questions, and excellent strategies for parenting teens that can be applied in any family or situation. The Author asks challenging questions in each chapter but also reminds the reader of God's grace in the process. I would highly recommend all parents read this book and ponder the questions as they approach and navigate the teen years. She also reminds us it is never too late to start. My girls are 18 and 21 and I am still learning and growing and applying new principles as we transition into new stages of parenting.

SALLY MARCUS CONROY

Certified Life Coach, Georgia, USA

Impressive and powerful!

I found "Raising Today's Teens. Are you ready?" easy to read and understand, it is very authentic and genuine. It also highlights the issues with raising kids in general - not just teens, making it very relatable to Parenting for all ages. It is a well written and engaging book.

BARBARA ENYENIHI

Norwich, UK

The author has a wonderful way of reminding us that our role as parents is a pivotal one in the life of our teens. In an age of easy access to information, we remain the greatest influence on them for a period of time. We must, therefore, uphold this time as a priority, ensuring that we are role modelling the right behaviours, balancing age-appropriate independence and the loving nurture that only a parent can give.

YEKEMI OTARU

Bestselling Author, Chancellor-elect at UWS, Founder: Business Scotland

It is a conversational, friendly, and yet practical and insightful guide to raising teenagers in today's world. The reader takes you on a parental self-discovery journey, the examples and anecdotes are eerily familiar to the extent where it almost seems like she had access to a big brother cam in your household. Simply put, this book is ammunition to parenting done right—a must-read for all parents and to be parents of teenagers.

DR. OSAGIE

Convener Berean Bible Meeting, USA

RAISING TODAY'S TEENS
ARE YOU READY?

AIMA AWENLIMOBOR

RAISING TODAY'S TEENS

Copyright © 2021 by Aima Awenlimobor

The right of the author has been asserted by her in accordance with the copyright writing, designs and patent act of the United Kingdom.

A catalogue copy of this book is available in the British Library.

All rights reserved. No part of this book may be reproduced, stored or transmitted by any means whether auditory, graphic, mechanical, or electronic without the written permission of the author, except in the case of brief excerpts used in critical articles and reviews. Unauthorised reproduction of any part of this work is illegal and is punishable by law.

Unless otherwise noted, the author and the publisher make no explicit guarantees as the accuracy of the information contained in this book may differ based on individual experiences and context.

For enquiries, email: raisingtodaysteens@outlook.com

ISBN: 9798477875184

DEDICATION

I dedicate this book to my parents Rt Hon. Chev (Engr) A. A. Ikheloa and Dame D. E Ikheloa, who held nothing back in bringing up my siblings and me. They showered us with love and equipped us with everything needed to lead successful adult lives.

Also to parents all over the world who walk the parenting journey relentlessly, determined to succeed even with the challenges they face.

Lastly to my husband who has been and continues to be my biggest advocate and my children who continue to challenge me to be the best version of myself.

CONTENTS

	Foreword	11
	Introduction	15
1	Being A Parent	21
2	Generation Z & The Younger Generation	35
3	Parenting Considerations	47
4	Parenting in Today's World	79
5	The God Factor	115
6	Summary and Conclusion	125
	Acknowledgements	129
	Endnotes	130

FOREWORD

Parenting is a privilege and one of the most rewarding full-time jobs on earth. With this privilege comes a huge task. I wish Parenting 101 course was offered in college.

I completely enjoyed reading this book that's based on lived experiences because Aima's practical examples resonate with me. Raising Today's Teens has given me unique insights at the right time. It couldn't have come at a much better time.

Like the author, I have three lovely children (a boy and two girls) with three distinct personalities and like many other parents, I'm always trying to find the right balance.

FOREWORD

One of the many issues Aima deals head-on with in this book is overparenting. Am I too hard? Am I too soft? Is this the right way? Have I made the right decision? These questions and many more flood my heart daily as I deal with my children. Seeing them on the pages of this book makes me realise I am not alone.

I also love the nuggets Aima provided in this book. They help make parenting an enjoyable experience.

My greatest takeaway from this book is how it's made me meditate on my family values and how important it is to remind ourselves of them, live our lives by these values because they are our road map and they guide us on our paths through life as individual members of our families.

I implore every parent to read Raising Today's Teens to discover what parenting really is and how one can navigate the 'hard' path easily.

This book deserves success, not only for Aima but for every parent who desires to do parenting the right way. I'm convinced that Aima is here to rescue parenthood. I also feel honoured for the opportunity to write the foreword to such an amazing, timely and sanity-saving book. I enjoyed it and I wish every parent does too.

OLA OLALEYE
Founder & President
The Esther's Company
(Nominee, Queens Award for Voluntary Services 2021)

INTRODUCTION

At what age could you say you have successfully raised your children? Would that be when they get into primary school? Or is that too early? Let us say when they get into the university or better still when they are done with their university or any higher education.

What about the children who do not pursue higher education but decide to learn a trade or start a business? Would you say you have successfully raised your children when they have excelled in their chosen trade or become successful in that business venture?

Some would say when the children become independent or when they get married and start raising their own children. Or when the children too, have successfully raised their children.

INTRODUCTION

I can go on and on because there are other scenarios some parents would favour, and I wonder if there is a right or wrong answer. I believe it all depends on individual perspectives and definitions of success which can differ from one person to another.

Let us not dwell on a definition of success but on the process of raising a child because in that process lies your success.

Parents deserve to give themselves a pat on the back after each milestone in a child's life instead of putting undue pressure on themselves. Raising children is not an easy task and is most certainly not a day's job. As parents (mums and dads) we need to do our best and then rest assured that we have sown the right seeds.

In my parenting journey so far, I have been faced with so many challenges, experienced a lot of victories, made so many mistakes along the way and learnt various lessons from them. Through it all, I have cried tears of joy and tears of frustration.

My husband and I have three fantastic children and could not ask for any better. However, even in all the beauty and joy that parenthood brings, there have been times I wished for a solo holiday or maybe, just a few days of alone time away from my home.

This sounds funny, right? Or maybe not, because you too might have experienced this at some point. Count yourself lucky if you can't relate to this.

A few years ago, after the end of my last maternity leave, I had to travel to a different town for some days for my "return to work" training. I felt so much relief just being away from home and leaving the children with my lovely husband.

I had heard people say how they needed to take some time away from home, but I never fully understood what they meant as I had never felt the need to do so before the "return to work" episode and to date, I still feel a bit guilty that I felt that good having some time off. However, I am learning never to feel guilty if I need to take a break and neither should you.

INTRODUCTION

In this book, I have put together challenges I have faced from my perspective as a mother; the mistakes I might have made, strategies I implemented and the results I got. This book will help families with children or those who plan to have children become better prepared for the teenage years.

It will also help those who struggle, particularly with raising teenagers, dealing with all the mood swings, the desire to be heard, the identity struggle and all that come with children transitioning from pre-teen to the teenage years.

Raising Today's Teens provides tips for parents who are confused with their teens and want to ensure positive parenting techniques; tips on how to look inwards and not always at the child because a child's behaviour often is a function of his or her environment.

This book also teaches that parenting is a journey; it's not a one rule fits all affair. As a parent, you will find in this book, the encouragement you need to carry on until you push through your parenting struggles as you are not alone on this journey.

It would also help future parents or parents with younger children avoid certain mistakes and misconceptions and be better equipped for the journey ahead.

Undoubtedly, I would have had things a bit easier and made fewer mistakes if I had some insights into parenting in today's world before I started my own journey.

If you are still wondering what it means to raise children in the world we live in today, you are in the right place. Go ahead and enjoy reading.

BEING A PARENT

What is parenting? My definition of parenting is the ability to nurture your children into being the best of themselves, to be happy and confident individuals and to become effective members of society.

Parenting is a full-time job, and it is important that parents first and foremost look after themselves to ensure they are in the best frame to look after their children. There is a need for parents to prioritise their health and wellbeing as a healthy, well-rested parent is in a better position to have a better influence on their children.

Think about your 9-5 job and how today's employers focus on ensuring everyone gets a chance to take a break during the day.

It is a known fact that people are more productive when they get some time away from their workstation to get some air, relax and recharge. This is also needed in the home.

Children are great imitators of those around them. According to psychologist Albert Bandura, children can learn by observing the actions of others.[i]

If you are a parent who is constantly tired, stressed out, juggling so many things and you do not take the time to intentionally model good behaviour to your children, they will not get to learn much from you. They will miss observing and imitating the best from you.

I understand that in today's world and with modern-day demands, both parents are entangled in the rat race, trying to ensure a better quality of life for the family. While there is nothing wrong with striving for the best we can for our families, we need to ensure that we do not lose sight of the task of raising our children.

We are the custodians of our children. They have been given to us to nurture and we might think we have the luxury of time as parents. But very quickly, before we realise it, these children will become adults and will move out and build their own families.

When this happens—it will happen—will you be content knowing that you did your best in raising your children and equipping them for life's challenges? Would you have equipped them with the ability to build their own homes and raise their own children? Or, will you wonder how differently they would have turned out if you did more? Do you want to live the rest of your life regretting not spending enough time with your children; not giving them the best of yourself?

I often hear parents complain about a child's behaviour and to be honest, I raise my hands to admit I have done the same. But we fail to realise no child is born with bad behaviour. Every behaviour is learnt and influenced in some way and at some point, from the different environments children are exposed to. So, if children are not born with certain bad behaviours, what is responsible for the negative behaviours portrayed by the children?

People are a product of a combination of their nature and nurture. Genetics play a role in a child's nature. This means the child could have similar traits (inherited) to a family member; most often, the parents. As the saying goes: "an apple does not fall far from the tree." Nurture (not inherited) also begins from the home. Societal influences have a role to play in nurturing a child and influencing who a person becomes. A child raised with strong family values stands a better chance in today's world in dealing with societal issues and vices.

Let's take a closer look at understanding what family values are.

Values and Responsibilities

Every family should have core values. And parents should aim to instil these values in their children from a young age. There is a popular saying that: "he that stands for nothing can fall for anything." What does this mean?

If you have no values, it is easy for confusion to set in.

Family values are principles upheld within the family. They could be cultural, religious, moral, ethical, social, and even political or economic.

Values alone can be described as principles a person believes to be important.

Cambridge dictionary describes values as:

> *the principles that help you to decide what is right and wrong, and how to act in various situations.[ii]*

Oxford Learner's dictionary describes family values, on the other hand, as:

> *beliefs about what is right, wrong, or important in life that people often learn from their families, typically the importance of high moral standards in the traditional family unit of mother, father, and children. In the United States, family values are strongly associated with conservative Christian values.*

Organisations also have core values. Take a moment to think about your day job, for example, and the core values of the organisation you work for. Your employers make it a priority to ensure staff are aware of the core values and abide by them. This is reflected in the work ethics, patterns, and behaviours.

Sharing your core values with your children in the home would ensure they become 'family values' that every family member strives to abide by.

I am a Christian and I hold dearly my Christian values. These values have helped and continue to help define who I am and how I live my life. It is my responsibility as a parent to introduce my values to my children because values affect behaviour and character.

Christian values cover many areas such as faith, love, forgiveness, obedience, self-control, respect, honesty, patience etc.

What values do you hold dear? Are your children familiar with your values? Do you portray your values in your behaviour and character? These are questions to ponder on as you read through this book.

As parents, it is our responsibility to look after our children. We need to guide and protect them from societal vices and wrong ideologies during the early stages of their development and sometimes we need to protect them from themselves. They are young and mostly naive and vulnerable. They are children and lack the years of experience that we have. And one of the ways to guide them is to use our value system.

There is a popular quotation from the Bible that states:

"Train up a child in the way he should go and when he is old, he will not depart from it."[iii]

How many times do you teach or train your child in a day?

The quotation implies that it is the parents' responsibility to train a child. Unfortunately, in today's world, a lot of parents leave the responsibility of training their children to schoolteachers, guidance counsellors or even religious leaders because of several reasons. That is not how it should be.

Some parents provide food, shelter, and the basic needs of their children. After doing this, they believe their job is done. Fathers are content being the breadwinners in some instances and believe that any training required should be done by the mothers. But a lot has changed in the world we live in today. Mothers are also busy trying to support their husbands financially and building their own careers. They are mostly too tired to bother about intentionally raising their children. And as parents get busier, there are many available options to help with the children.

Some parents are so quick to whisk their children away to boarding schools as soon as possible to avoid the day-to-day responsibilities of raising the children, and probably get the much-needed free time to do other things.

Do not get me wrong, boarding schools have their benefits and might work for some families. I attended a boarding school at some point during my secondary school education. However, I made up my mind never to send my children to boarding schools. This is a personal choice because I want to be able to impact them as much as possible and most importantly because I want to be able to spend as much time with them while they are still young. I can only achieve this if I am around them enough. I want to make our time together count and ensure every discussion and time together is a teachable moment.

Training does not have to come in the form of a classroom chair and desk arrangement.

Training can happen anywhere and at any time.

Training can take place in the kitchen, in the living room, at the movies together, on the way to school, while shopping and even laughing together and so on.

Here again, I ask:

What are your core family values? Do your children know what they are?

It is your responsibility as a parent to endeavour to imbibe family values in your children by exposing them to those values from a young age and intentionally teach, while modelling, these values.

Modelling has been deliberately mentioned as it is important that our children see us do what we say we believe or value. For example, we cannot say smoking is bad for the health and begin or continue to smoke in the presence of the children.

Oh yes, that example is easy, right? I mean, who does that? How about this? We cannot tell our children it is not nice to yell at their siblings when all we do is yell at them all day. Does this sound like you? I have been there, so it is not a blame and shame game.

These are the things to bear in mind when intentionally raising your children. What kind of behaviours do you model? Do you say one thing and do the other?

It is therefore important to note that parenting is a serious business and not a part-time job where you can take a break and pick up where you left off. Parenting is no mean feat, but it is the most rewarding job in the world. And to think that for a job that is so important there is no formal training.

With no formal training, how then do we get it right? Parents have got to pull together all their experiences as well as learn on the job to ensure they do a good job. How exciting!

I believe my responsibility as a parent is to raise children who would become responsible, confident, and happy adults. My responsibility is also to ensure they become the best version of themselves.

Note the use of the phrase best version of themselves. This is easier said than done.

Have you ever been inclined to compare one child with another and say, "Oh, your brother just did this, why can't you do the same?" Or "See what your cousin just accomplished, what about you?"

Do we tend to compare our children with their peers?

A lot of times, we may not mean any harm because we do it with good intentions to encourage that child to do better. But does this help the child become the best version of him or herself or does he or she end up trying to be like someone else? It is tricky right? Where do we draw the line? How would you feel if your children compared you to other parents? Food for thought.

It's also parents' responsibility to provide a child's basic needs until they reach adulthood. Food, clothing, shelter and so on. Parents need to provide a stable and enabling environment for their children in other to raise stable and empowered adults.

And here comes another question. What kind of adults are you raising? Or what kind of adults do you want to raise? Does your answer include:

- Independent
- Stable
- Achieving
- Generous
- Kind
- Peaceful

And the list goes on. But note again that no matter what your answer is, your children should be the best version of themselves and not a counterfeit of someone else.

Everyone is unique and has something special about them. You want to know what it is that makes them unique so you can help them to harness this. You also want to know their weaknesses so you can help them strengthen these areas.

In essence, teach your children how to handle themselves. Or simply put, teach them to be the best of themselves. There is no perfect person, but every child was born to be perfect just the way they are.

GENERATION Z & THE YOUNGER GENERATION

Not too long ago I came across the term *Generation Z* for the first time while watching a television programme and I was curious. I did some research in my usual manner because I wanted to find out more.

Over the years various generations have been given various names. There was the *Silent Generation* for children born between 1928 and 1945; then the *Baby Boomers* which applied to children born between the years of 1946 and 1964; *Generation X* for children between 1965 and 1980; *Millennials* born between 1981 and 1996; and more recently *Generation Z* for children born between 1997 and 2012. There is also the *Alpha Generation*, those born between the early 2010s to those that will be born in the mid-2020s.[iv]

I noticed how people were classified based on the era they were born. Based on the dates stated above, *Generation Z* would be children between the ages of 9 and 24, as of the year of publishing this book, 2021. This is a generation that cannot be ignored in this book because today's teen falls into this category.

There is no telling what Generation Alpha and the ones after it would be like, but *Generation Z* is already leaving its mark in the world.

Generation Z is supposedly the most informed generation yet. It is the generation that has access to so much information, readily available at its fingertips. This is the generation that was born into the internet world with some of its members having their first iPads/internet gadgets as early as the age of 4 or even earlier. This generation has had a huge impact on fashion, politics, and societal trends in general.

There are many benefits of having information readily available, some would say. While I do not disagree, we must also realise that there are some disadvantages.

Two of my children fall within *Generation Z*. From my interactions with them and other children in their age group, I have noticed some possible disadvantages of being raised with so much access to information.

It is no news that one of the biggest challenges of parenting today is how to effectively manage screen time and social media access. As parents to members of *Generation Z*, we couldn't have learned the skill to deal with this from our parents who didn't have this challenge while we were growing up.

While parents struggle with this, members of *Generation Z* in some cases, tend to have a false sense of confidence in their knowledge/wisdom. Some of them believe that whatever they need to know or learn can easily be accessed online. Because the internet or should I say the 'information hub' is just a fingertip away, some of these children no longer have that need to work hard in certain cases. They rely more on the internet and cannot imagine a life without it.

Having easy access to information is good, but it also exposes children to the wrong kind of information.

"I can just 'Google it', mum," is now a popular phrase when conversing with pre-teens and teenagers.

How many Google sources are verified? How many information sources share the same values as your family? Confusion easily sets in when family values and ethics do not align with what children find online.

"It's okay to do so. I checked online and everyone does it." You probably have heard this phrase before.

Where I grew up, there was a popular saying that: "The community raises the child." This was a good thing at the time. Where parents' responsibilities stopped or paused because they weren't around the children, the community's began. Children knew that even though Mum or Dad was not always present, there would always be one overzealous relative who would ensure that Mum and Dad found out about the children's deeds or the relative who took over the role of parenting temporarily to ensure the family values aren't compromised. And it wasn't only relatives, but any older person in the children's immediate environment because the community values mirrored the family values in a lot of instances. So, children mostly had to be well behaved even in the absence of their parents.

In the present day, our children have more access to communities online, different from the kind of communities we grew up in. We must ask:

What kind of communities are they keying into? Do these mostly faceless communities share the same values with your family?

Some might argue that these communities aren't exactly faceless because they have names and photos. I call them faceless because these are people not known personally to the children or the family members in some cases. These are people the children would most likely never meet. These people's values might be completely different from your family values.

While we are talking about these online communities, and you're already thinking: "I could just keep them away from social media or monitor their activities." Please, reconsider. How long can you possibly do this? As much as it is important to guide your children, particularly with social media access and all the vices they could be exposed to on the internet, there are so many seemingly harmless channels that children are constantly exposed to.

Information technology and easy access to information make a lot of difference to the way our children see the world and themselves which is different from the way we saw the world and ourselves as children.

Does this mean that the methods our parents used in raising us would not necessarily work in raising our children?

Do we need to tweak a few things or stick with what we know from our parents tried and trusted methods?

If we decide to create new methods, how do we know that these new methods would yield positive results? Children are children, right? Does it matter if they are being raised in a different world than we were? Why shouldn't what works for one child work for the other?

When it comes to raising children, the questions are endless.

Societal Influences

As time progresses, the world changes. From one century to the next, so much has changed. Today's world is very different from the one I grew up in. Cultures have been diluted. Religious organisations in some parts of the world have almost become laughable. There is so much confusion and crisis in the world and it is so easy for children to be confused.

Certain behaviours were once considered taboos and unacceptable in most—if not all—cultures, years ago.

Today, those same behaviours have become acceptable in most parts of the world and in some cases, they are the popular and celebrated choice.

The society we live in goes a long way to shape the ways a child thinks and influences to a large extent who they become. For this reason, we ask:

- How do we shield our children from societal ills?
- Do we completely shield them as they grow and allow them to face the real world when they are adults?
- Would they have what it takes to make the right choices in adulthood if they are completely shielded?
- Should we expose them wisely to the ills of society and teach them how to handle society as it is?
- Do we even know how to do the above?
- Can we answer questions intelligently when our children ask them?
- Do we have enough information to do so?

As a Christian, I ensure that I teach my children Christian values but:

- Is it right to rely solely on my Christian values?
- What about simple ethics and morals?
- Do they all fit in?

These are questions some parents might have and again I wonder if there is one simple answer.

Expectations and Reality

I have pondered over so many questions repeatedly and wondered if I was doing enough. I have come to realise that I can only do my best as a parent and not worry about what I do not have control over. While I understand that today's society is different from what it was years ago, I also realise that there has always been some element of societal ills.

My parents might not have always got it right, but I can confidently state without any doubt that they did their best and I want my children to be able to state the same when they are older.

Children have been given free will. As they grow older, they will make certain life choices. As parents, it is our responsibility to ensure they are well equipped to make fully informed decisions and by God's grace, the right choices when they need to.

The world is constantly changing. There is no guarantee what the world would be like in 2031 for example, but like with any good building, a solid foundation is paramount to ensure the building can withstand various weather conditions. A solid foundation is all we need to give our children.

Children are adorable and we expect them to be perfect but, they cannot always be perfect. They will make mistakes, sometimes they may cause us headaches, they could even make us shed tears but like the adage mentioned in an earlier chapter "an apple doesn't fall far from the tree." Our children are often not so different from us. If we look back, we probably gave our parents headaches at some point too. We probably made our mums yell so loud sometimes the way our children make us yell at times.

Oftentimes, I feel like calling my mum to ask for forgiveness when I think of the times I made her yell. I now understand how difficult her task was and I wish I could go back in time to make it easier for her. Nevertheless, we must try to take it easy with our children.

Are you too hard on your children? Try to take a step back. Understand that they are children and cannot act like sensible and responsible adults. Some of the phases the children are currently in today would likely pass if handled the right way. Do not have unrealistic expectations and endeavour not to dwell on little things.

Here is another lesson I have learnt over the years:

> Do not focus on your children's weaknesses. Such focus will make the weaknesses more prominent. Instead, focus on their strengths and the weaknesses will gradually take a back sit.

3

PARENTING CONSIDERATIONS

I mentioned earlier that, children are a function of their nature and nurture (in other words, their environment). No child is born 'bad', but they could have challenging traits; strong-willed, opinionated, difficult, etc. These traits—which some parents complain about—can be channelled correctly instead of being suppressed.

Just like us, children have various temperaments and personality traits, and it is the responsibility of parents to take the time to understand them. If you have more than one child, do not expect them to be the same. What works for child A may not necessarily work for child B. So, quit the comparisons and quit trying to apply the same methods for all your children. Each child is unique; it is important that parents understand this, to be able to bring out the best in their children.

Children's temperament and genetic makeup play a big role in who they become. Their environment also plays an important role, and this is where nurture can have an upper hand if properly done, especially where parents are faced with challenging personalities.

The first environment where children's learning begins is the home and this environment raises these questions:

- What are they exposed to in the home?
- What behaviour do they see in the home?
- Do you model the right behaviours, or do you expect them to do as you say and not as you do?
- Do you tell them your values but do not model them?

Like I stated in a previous chapter, children are observant and incredibly good at imitation. They see what their parents do and naturally copy.

I am a recovering *yeller*. There was a period in my home when my children could not speak to each other without yelling. My oldest would yell at my middle child who in turn would yell at the youngest. It was complete chaos. Everyone was yelling. I could not understand why they couldn't keep their voices down. Whenever someone called me on the phone, they would hear my children yelling in the background.

When I began my journey to strip myself of some bad parenting habits, such as yelling, I took the children with me on the journey. One of the things I did was to create a 'Yeller Chart'. The 'Yeller Chart' kept a daily record of the yelling in the home to find out who yelled the most. This chart was followed with a challenge in the home to significantly reduce the yeller count and the person who was the most improved over a period won the challenge.

To my surprise, my 6-year-old and I had the highest yeller counts per day. I was determined to change this. I ensured that I practised what I preached and intentionally made that change. My goal was to prove to the children that mummy was not perfect and can improve. Yelling was something I struggled with for years, so I made them my accountability partners. My determination paid off and now yelling in my home is a rare occurrence.

Parents are not perfect, and children can see that. Children can also see when you make that conscious effort to do better. They learn and can apply it to their lives. Children want to see you practice what you preach. It is always beneficial to model the sort of behaviours you want to see for them to follow.

Today's children are smart and generally more informed than we were as children. They know when you are in the wrong but pretend to be in the right. If you are a parent and you have not been intentional about modelling good behaviour, now is the time to start. If you think it is already too late to model good behaviour, take this from me: it is never too late to make changes.

Start teaching them to own their own mistakes by owning yours. Stop pretending to be perfect. Don't hide your mistakes when you make them and let them see the process of change and the journey you go through to make amends. That in itself is a learning point for the children.

Parenting Responsibilities

Both parents have a role to play in raising children. Raising a child is not just a mother's job as is believed in some cultures. The two people who came together to procreate, are the same people with the responsibility to raise the child. The roles of a dad and mum are unique as they have different impacts on the children. One cannot play the role of the other and I do not believe this is optional. Where possible, both parents should have an active role in a child's upbringing.

Our society also has many homes with single parents. I believe the way around this could be to find a father figure or mother figure to provide their support. This person can be a close relative or a trusted friend who the child will be accountable to. So, other than just the single mum or dad, there should be somebody else the child can learn from. This helps create some needed balance.

When assigning parenting responsibilities in the home, there is no need to enforce traditional roles to the mother or the father. Some people believe the mother's role is fully domesticated—responsible for cleaning the house, cooking the meals, and caring for the children—while the father is solely responsible for financial matters.

We live in a different world today and these traditional roles are gradually fading away. We cannot hold on to traditions if we want to ensure that our children can function effectively in a changing world.

Couples should consider their strengths and function in their areas of strength. If a role is a weak point for one but a strength for the other, switch roles and let the children learn. That is how the home would maintain maximum functionality without too much pressure on one parent.

If Dad is a better cleaner than Mum, then Dad should take charge of cleaning the home and let the children learn from him. If Mum is better at changing the light bulbs, let Mum do so and let the children learn from her. If Dad is more patient and effective with the children's homework, then do not wait for Mum to get through all her chores and still sit with the children to do homework. If Dad is a better organiser let him go ahead and organise the home while Mum supports. If Dad is a better cook, no need to wait for Mother's Day to prepare that nice meal; do it as often as you are available and let the children observe and learn. If

Mum is better at disciplining the children, let her do so and let Dad support her.

We are all wired differently and what comes easy to one parent might not come easy to the other. Stop for a moment and ponder where your strength lies as a parent.

It is okay to have traditional roles to ensure some order in the home but as couples grow together, their strengths and weaknesses become obvious and as time goes on, instead of standing by while one partner struggles to get it right with whatever traditional role she/he has been assigned, the home would be a better place if the other partner is flexible enough to take some of the burdens off where possible.

Enforcing traditional roles all the time could lead to one partner becoming burnt out and the effect of this can rub off on the children. A burnt-out parent cannot be effective in the home.

Consider the case of a mum with a demanding job. She works longer hours than the dad and gets home late on some days. In some cases, she is still expected to get home, drop her bags and head straight to the kitchen to prepare dinner for the family. The children and the dad—who have been home hours earlier—would sit in the lounge watching their favourite TV programme.

Family time and rest are important for everyone. But for this mum, she would want to get the meal on the table as quickly as possible and head off to bed. She is not only tired after a busy day; she is probably also hungry but too tired to have a meal. If this happens often this mum will get mentally and physically drained. She will become irritable, short-tempered and get to that point where she can no longer be an effective parent to her children.

A parent must be in the right mental frame to be able to intentionally raise children. This could also happen to dads as mums aren't the only ones who get burnt out. The key is to work together as parents to get the balance right for both parties to ensure effective parenting.

Overparenting

As parents, we love our children dearly and one thing we struggle with is letting go. We struggle with the fear of not looking after them enough or not being the best parent and we tend to want to shield them from as much harm as possible. As a result, we 'over-parent' or shield them excessively.

Instead of overparenting children, parents can learn age-appropriate parenting. The technique I use for my 6-year-old does not have to be the same as what I use with my 13-year-old. The technique I use for child A irrespective of age does not have to be the same as what I use for child B.

Some children are more independent than others and would thrive better if given more responsibilities. Others might not be wired the same way and might need a bit more guidance in certain areas. We must understand our children, their personalities, strengths, and weaknesses to understand what techniques will work best for each child and help us adjust for the weaknesses.

PARENTING CONSIDERATIONS

One of the sure ways of understanding children is spending time with them, chatting with them, and listening to them. Take some time to reflect on this.

When was the last time you had a heart-to-heart conversation with your child? I do not mean a one-way conversation where you tell your child the dos and don'ts but a two-way discussion, where your child can also tell you what and how he or she feels and thinks, while you listen.

The more you do this—have two-way discussions—the more you understand your children and who they are becoming as they grow older. With your understanding of one child, you can determine how much parenting that child needs. Does he need constant reminders in certain areas? Does she need some space to show you what she can do? Or will you keep on helping your children out with everything?

I'll give a practical example. I have two daughters and I usually fix their hair in the mornings. Brush, oil and sometimes put in a bun as required. As the older girl grew, she would say "Mum, I can do it myself," and I would return, "Just let me do it, I'll be quicker." This went on for a while. She kept complaining and no longer appreciated my efforts at fixing her hair.

When I went around to get her hair done, she put up disagreeable countenances, followed by constant whining that she was hurting. This used to be a lovely mother and daughter activity that we both enjoyed but it had become an activity she no longer appreciated. I had to let go, albeit painfully. When I did, she came up with other creative ways of fixing her hair and I was impressed. Sometimes, she still asks for my help when she needs it and I happily oblige.

Another example is picking out the children's clothes. My 6-year-old would want to pick her choice of clothes and I let her do so most of the time. I only bother with her choice of clothes when we have an important outing or when I must consider the weather and the appropriateness of her outfit.

There are dangers of overparenting. These include:
- Unhealthy dependency on parents.
- Inability of children to make their own choices.

- Fear of failure.
- Inability to handle or rise from failure.
- Inability to effectively manage responsibilities.
- Low self-esteem as children may become unable to trust their own judgements.
- Rebellion and a feeling of being choked as they struggle to be heard and are not allowed to have a voice.

Children's desire to be more independent is a natural part of growing up and shouldn't be frowned upon. Instead, they should be given age-appropriate independence and responsibility. We should intentionally let our children mature under our supervision so that when they are outside the home, they can handle themselves.

Letting go of some things that are not too important and giving the control of little things that are of little consequence builds the child's self-esteem and self-worth and allows us to assess their level of maturity and areas where more support is needed.

Are you overparenting? Your response to the following questions can help you answer the above question. Remember this is not a blame game. I have been in these shoes.

- Are you constantly in a power struggle over every little thing?
- Do you find it difficult to apportion tasks or responsibilities and let the children just get on with it?
- Are you overprotective and afraid to see the children hurt or fail?
- Are you constantly micromanaging everything they do out of fear that they might get it wrong?
- Do you struggle to understand age-appropriate independence?

If your answer to any of these is yes, now is the time to pull back and re-evaluate. While you love your children, the last thing you want to do is suffocate them with your love.

Shielding

Overparenting goes hand in hand with shielding. I once discussed this with an uncle who is a seasoned Social Worker in the UK. He was the first person to draw my attention to the term 'Shielding' concerning parenting and I did some follow up research.

Shielding occurs when parents keep the children away from doing age-appropriate activities for fear that they might get hurt, make mistakes, or be exposed to societal vices and so on.

Parents want to restrict the children's play in the park, so they don't fall and hurt their knees. We keep them indoors, so they don't mix with bad company.

Parents usually have good intentions but the downside of this is that shielding prevents children from maturing naturally. Shielding does not allow children to develop properly at the right age and they miss out on making age-appropriate mistakes.

When children get to an age where parents can no longer shield them, they may not be properly equipped to make the right choices. At this stage we find young adults making juvenile choices and mistakes that they should have made and learnt from at a younger age. Making mistakes is a part of growing up and a learning process, hence, it should not be completely frowned upon.

As a result of shielding, some children become unable or unwilling to venture into the world without fear. Some prefer to go far away from home once they get the opportunity just so they can be far from the prying eyes of their parents, thus exposing themselves to unnecessary challenges. Other children who have been shielded, thrust themselves into the world once they get the slightest opportunity, feeling as though they have missed out on what their peers experienced and wanting so badly to catch up. This might lead to mistakes with serious consequences.

Instead of shielding them, teach them. Children should know in the real world, when they are not with Mum and Dad, they could fall off their bikes and hurt their knees and it won't be the end of the world. They might get in contact with a bad company, but they need to know how to fend them off if required and not be influenced negatively.

Every child is different; know your children. Instil the right values in them when they are younger. So that once they get to the right age you will be more confident in their ability to make the right choices. However, if they make mistakes, it won't be the end of the world because you would have taught them to pick themselves up and to learn from their mistakes.

I am not an advocate for letting children do as they please at any age. I would rather take the time to understand their age and the stages of their development and allow appropriate developmental activities that would build them into well-rounded adults.

Once you have imbibed and understood what is required for your children's development, the biggest challenge will be to find the right balance and knowing when to let go.

Finding the Right Balance

Through the years, I have developed in my parenting journey and as I stated earlier, I have made some mistakes and learnt from them. If I knew at the beginning of my journey what I know now, I might have done some things a little differently.

I used to be a perfectionist. Everything had to be perfect in the home. Everywhere had to be tidy, spotless carpets, stainless walls all the time. I used to pride myself in having a tidy home and sometimes, you would wonder if there were children living in the home as they were not allowed to make a mess and if they ever did, they had to clean up immediately. Basically, they were not allowed to be children.

I started to realise something was wrong when we went out for family meals at restaurants and the children would refuse to sit in the restaurants if there was any spot or stain on the carpet underneath the tables or anywhere near the tables, worse if the chairs had any stains or marks on them.

I had so many embarrassing moments trying to clean up tables at restaurants if there was a tiny stain just to get my children to agree to sit for a meal. I couldn't blame them; they just couldn't stand anything with a stain. They'd been taught by their mum that everything and everywhere had to be spotless. They behaved the same way when we visited friends and an embarrassed mum would struggle to hide the reason behind their decision to stand and not sit. I would stylishly find the cleanest part of the room and lure them there to avoid further embarrassment.

There is nothing wrong with being tidy and having a squeaky-clean home, but I realised it gave my children a false sense of the world. The world is not an extremely tidy place and if my home appeared 'spotless' my children would naturally be uncomfortable anywhere that wasn't the same.

One of the things I have since changed in my journey is my home. This is a difficult example as one would expect cleanliness to be a good thing. But this all comes down to how it was done, to what extent and how much importance was attached to it above other things and so on.

All I did was make specific changes without having an untidy home. I stopped making a big deal if I noticed a stain on my white doors for example. I stopped rushing to pick up every dirt on the carpet every other second. I stopped making a big deal of every stain or spill after a meal on the dining table.

Balance is important in raising children and once I noticed the effect my 'tidiness' was having on my children I fixed it and since the changes, the embarrassing restaurant scenarios have gradually become a rare occurrence.

Parents sometimes try too hard. We buy our children the nicest clothes, so they look well-groomed. We buy them whatever they ask for, so they lack nothing. We give them choices of meals, so they never go hungry.

We basically ensure they have all the comfort we can provide. This isn't bad, don't get me wrong. But at what point do the children get to know, that they might encounter a different world outside the home?

They might want nice clothes but might not always be able to afford them or might have other more important priorities. They might not always have the option of their favourite meal but should still be able to avoid going hungry by accepting what is available. They might even go hungry for a while if there is no food at that point and it would not be the end of the world.

Balance is a word I love to use. If we can find the right balance it makes a lot of difference. When next you offer to make a separate meal for child A because he/she does not like what is served for dinner, think about what you are teaching your child. It might be okay to do this sometimes, but do you do this all the time?

And if you are shielding, the next time you try to hold them back from going out to play with friends, think about the benefits and the dangers. The next time you hold a child from running in the park, think about the worst that could happen. Should they fall and hurt their knee, would they be more careful next time? Try to find the right balance.

There are age-appropriate restrictions and age-appropriate privileges as I already stated. It is a parent's responsibility to know when to allow certain privileges and when to enforce certain restrictions. Some of these depend on your child's personality and maturity.

In our goal to raise perfect children, we tend to expect too much from our children and end up putting them under undue pressure. They must be the best at school, they have to be at the top of their class and whenever they don't attain this, they'd have some explaining to do. This might sound like what some of us experienced as children. You are lucky if you did not have to be the best in your class growing up.

When I was growing up, it was the norm. As a child, my parents expected me to always be the best (even though I didn't always achieve this). And so naturally, I expected the same from my children. But doing this ended up putting too much pressure on myself and on the child.

Don't get me wrong, there is nothing wrong with wanting your children to be great and have them work hard at school, but we need to know where to draw the line and understand our children's abilities.

There is nothing bad in working towards excellence. But it's not the end of the world if our children are not the best all the time. Don't put pressure on yourself and others in your home. It is unhealthy to compare one child with the other or to compare them with their peers outside the home.

Pushing your children too hard can affect their self-confidence, they might begin to doubt their abilities and even become parent pleasers. They might begin to depend on Mum and Dad's validation and in the absence of Mum and Dad, might seek validation elsewhere simply because that's how they know to validate themselves.

What do you expect from your children? Do you expect too much? Do you push them too hard? Do you have the right balance?

A little push here and little encouragement there and then an appreciation for their effort will go a long way to build their self-esteem. Teach your children to be proud of themselves irrespective of their achievements. And as you find the right balance, help them to find the same.

Parenting Challenges and the Right Approach

When my older children were younger, they went along with the rules I laid down. I taught them how to behave, what to do and what not to do. I taught them about values, behaviours and consequences of actions and it was a great time. But as they grew older, they began to ask questions. Why this? Why that? Why can't we do this? Why can't we go there? To be honest, I had all the answers. Or I thought I did. Most of my answers didn't make any sense to them, which got me thinking.

- Why did I do the things I did?
- Why did I have the rules I had?
- Was I trying so hard to shield them from societal ills?
- Was I being overprotective?
- Was I worried that they would make terrible mistakes?
- Had I done enough teaching and modelling when they were younger to trust their judgement as they grew older?
- Were they old enough to make the right judgement?
- Should I relax some of the home rules?
- When is the right time to relax these rules?
- Am I in essence overparenting my children?

PARENTING CONSIDERATIONS

I found myself in a confused state. For the first time, in all my years of being on the parenting journey, as my first two children transitioned into 'teenage hood', I didn't know what to do. I used to have everything figured out, but I had not planned for the teenage years.

I wrongly assumed that, like I did when growing up, my children would continue to go along with the laid down rules without asking questions. It dawned on me that I might have been a bit too strict with the rules and maybe a bit too rigid in enforcing them. Bedtime, homework time, phone usage, going out restrictions, social media etc.

My laid down rules were not that many, and they were necessary at the time based on their ages. But then, it appeared as though it might have been easier to go through the teenage phase if I didn't have so many rules.

I struggled because I did not know how to effectively manage the children without missing my purpose. I prayed hard about it because I was so confused. In this new place I found myself, I did not know how to walk with them without enforcing rules. I knew I taught them to be responsible, respectful, hardworking,

God-fearing and all that. The children knew all the rules in the book. But did I teach them to want—based on their decisions—to be or do these things or did I teach them to be all these because that's what Mum and Dad wanted?

I couldn't tell if that was a bad approach or if it was appropriate at the time. And there began a new challenge.

- How do I scale back and teach my children to want, to desire to be these things?
- Or how do I proceed to build on what they already knew so that it wasn't always about doing what Mum and Dad wanted?
- Was I too late to start or was I right on time?
- What was the right approach?

This is where so many parents get it wrong. That your children know what is right does not mean they will always choose the right path. Do they choose to do the right thing because you are watching or because that's what they want to do? I wanted my children to *choose* the right thing for themselves and this was where I struggled because rules did not work here.

As a young girl growing up in Nigeria, I knew so many people who were so-called 'saints' at home but outside the home, they were far from being saints. The first opportunity of freedom I and some of my peers had, was leaving home for the university, to live on the university campus and away from the prying eyes of our parents.

My peers and I were mostly from very responsible homes. However, I found out that several supposedly well brought up young people got involved in all sorts of vices because, for the first time, they were free to make their own choices. Choices that weren't right. For the first time, there was no one to judge them, watch them or even hold them accountable.

Today, we are parents. Do we want to raise children who would be 'saints' at home only? I want to know who my children are, even with every imperfection and every wrong choice. I want them to be themselves with me. I don't want them to feel the need to keep anything hidden from me. Most importantly, I want them to always feel the need to make the right choices irrespective of who is watching.

I wonder how many parents of supposedly well-behaved children go through a similar challenge. I also could have been referred to as a well brought up child but not all my choices were right. Peer pressure is real and while children may be shielded from that for a while, do they have what it takes to deal with it effectively when faced with the reality of it, especially in the absence of Mum and Dad?

I mentioned earlier that no child is born 'bad', but children go through different stages where they struggle to understand themselves. As they get older, they experience hormonal changes during puberty. Mood swings, body changes etc. are parts of the package that puberty brings. Going through this period, children may exhibit various unexpected behaviours. They may seek attention, cry for help, depending on what they are going through.

As parents, we must not judge or tag them, no matter how tempting that might be. Some children are labelled by their parents. "The troublesome child." "The problematic one." "The stubborn child." "The chatterbox." "The quiet one." And a whole lot of others.

Agreed, not all these labels have a negative undertone, but they tend to stick to the children, and they begin to see themselves as such. This makes it difficult for them to move away from that kind of behaviour which could have been just a phase in their lives. Oftentimes they see no reason to change and would settle for the labels. Even when they try to change, their efforts go unnoticed as everyone expects them to continue to behave according to the label.

It is important that we try to understand our children and tolerate them while they go through the various phases.

Unfortunately, as busy parents, we sometimes miss these stages, we do not recognise when our children are going through them, and we end up judging and name tagging, and in the process, we push the children away.

I started writing this book about a year ago at a time when I thought I had all the answers that relate to raising children. As I continued, my eyes got opened to a whole lot more and I realised that we are all on a continuous learning journey.

My 6-year-old, for example, is different from her older siblings. She is uniquely her own individual. If I applied the strategies I used for the older children on her, they wouldn't bring out the best in her.

As parents, we should know that we do not have all the answers, but we can reach out to other parents when or if we struggle. We can get information on how to handle various challenges when we arrive at stumbling blocks or when we have no clue about what we are doing.

We can read books or seek counsel to learn more. Do not keep repeating the same actions when you know it is not producing the desired results. Talk about demanding better results from a blunt axe! Get educated and creative. And don't forget that there is nothing like one rule fits all.

So, what is the right approach?

- Study your children and understand them.
- Know what you want to achieve.
- Know what kind of children you want to raise and start learning. Learn what you do not know—do not make the mistake of thinking you know it all.

- Keep the company of people who have been on the same journey so you can share ideas and ask questions.

Get yourself educated and be specific with your plans on how you want to raise your children. Do not rely on replicating how you were raised because we live in a different world today.

In the following chapters, I share practical tips that I have gathered, that have helped me navigate my parenting journey and while I am still in the process of navigating the teen years, these tips have made my path a lot clearer.

You may not have teenage children yet, but trust me, if anyone had told me three or four years ago that I would be looking to improve on my parenting style, I would have disagreed because my style worked perfectly for me until I got to the road bumps. Now I realise that you never know until you know, and we can never stop learning on this journey.

Other than the challenges of raising teenage children, which some parents truly do not encounter, these tips are also important for navigating relationships in general with the younger generation.

4

PARENTING IN TODAY'S WORLD

Parenting pre-teens and teenagers have undoubtedly been the most challenging period in my parenting journey so far.

I have a teenage son and daughter who are both highly intelligent but with different personalities. They have different temperaments, likes and dislikes. And because their ages aren't so far apart, I feel like I am dealing with twin teens but they have challenged me to be better.

It became clearer to me much recently that the same method of parenting was not going to be effective for both of them and it was important that I tweaked my approach for each child to get the best outcome and bring out the best in them.

To do this, I began to intentionally look after myself first—mentally and psychologically as I explained in the previous chapter—to ensure I am constantly aware of my own state of mind.

This is a very crucial step when dealing with teens. Your emotional state is easily transferable to your teens who are probably going through their own emotional battles. If you come across as emotionally unstable or mentally stressed, your teens will be unable to rely on you for support.

Also, it will be difficult for you as a parent to respond to their needs objectively and effectively. I found that whenever I was extremely tired or stressed from work, I did not have the patience to listen to my children or to notice their struggles. So, I made a conscious effort to cut out any stress generating factors in my immediate environment. I removed unnecessary distractions like worrying about every little thing around me and focused more energy on looking after myself. I took time out to relax and recoup after a busy spell and generally ensured I was doing fine all round.

Next, I became more intentional in modelling the right behaviours. I studied more to better understand the changes my children were experiencing to ensure I was better informed. This, of course, has made me more equipped for the journey ahead.

Culture and Balance

My next step was to return to the basics. I asked myself:

- Who am I?
- Who are we?
- What do we stand for?
- Where do we live?
- What's the predominant culture in the society we live in?
- What are the societal influences my children face at this age?
- What are the differences between the environment I grew up in and the environment they are being brought up in?

We are a Nigerian-British family living in the UK, with all three children born in the UK. Although our children are Nigerians as well as British, they have never lived in Nigeria.

I pondered on the questions and knew the answers would bring a new understanding. First, my husband and I are from Nigeria. Our Nigerian values had to count as the children had to be reminded of their origin and this provided some perspective for me. We could pick and choose the aspect of Nigerian and British culture we desired to adopt, which must align with our family values.

This cleared up certain areas of confusion and made certain discussions with the children easier. This is still a work in progress, but I knew we couldn't completely drop one culture to adopt the other. The good news is that we could get the best of both worlds. That sounds great but how does it work in reality?

I had to recognise that in my children's minds they were British citizens born to Nigerian parents. So, it might be difficult for them to completely identify with the Nigerian culture.

However, I understood the importance of ensuring they fully embrace their identity. I began to change that notion that they were solely British by slowly getting them to be more in tune with their Nigerian side.

I showed them how they could be proudly Nigerian and British at the same time without forcing it on them.

I showed them the cool things about their Nigerian culture. Connected them with some of their peers, and relatives to consciously link them to their Nigerian roots.

I also introduced Nigeria to our fun time, so that all they know about their country isn't all they see and hear on the news.

We started doing Nigerian games, quizzes, dressing up in Nigerian attire, learning Nigerian dances, discussing the culture, politics, history and so on. This helped me strengthen the Nigerian culture in the home. This also helped them to fully embrace their Nigerian side as they became more in tune with their roots.

Finding the balance is the tricky bit as they are mostly surrounded by the 'Britishness' of the society. But having a strong cultural background and knowing who they are, is important as children grow. This would ensure they understand their identity and therefore not see the need to conform or become someone else.

Having this strong cultural background boosts children's self-confidence and helps them better understand themselves and improves their choices. My children are Nigerian, and they are also British, and they are proud of both heritages.

If you live in a different society from your ethnic roots, find something that works for you. If you live in a society where culture isn't an issue, think about the children's exposure.

- Are they exposed to the right influences to ensure the right cultural values are imbibed?

- Do you want to ensure they do not lose who they are in the bid to follow the latest trends or popular fads?
- Do they know the importance of understanding who they are, their culture and beliefs and do they place the right value on this?
- Or are they more interested in following the culture in the movies they watch or the things they see on social media?

We must be intentional in ensuring they understand and value their culture as long as it is in line with our family values. This cannot be overemphasised. The world is a global village, and everyone wants to fit in, but it is easy to lose oneself in all that is going on. There is a popular saying, "He who stands for nothing will fall for anything."

Mindset Shift

How do we relate with our children? What kind of relationship do we have with them? Is it one built on trust, friendship, companionship or is it a more authoritarian parent-child relationship? Are we just the 'provider' type of parent who provides all they want/need, and our job is done?

I've often heard parents say, "I am my children's parent, not their friend," and "I do not have to be their friend to be a good parent."

I beg to disagree. And this is a conclusion I have drawn after carefully considering my experiences as a child and as a parent. Have you ever heard the saying, "Show me your friend and I'll tell you who you are?" Another saying is, "Show me your friend and I'd show you your future."

These popular sayings imply that people are a lot like those they hang around because traits and behaviours are easily learned or copied from people we spend a lot of our time with.

Motivational Speaker Jim Rohn said, "You're an average of the five people you spend most of your time with."

While some might argue that the average could span across more than five people, the point is that an individual is an average of the people he surrounds himself with or those he pays attention to.

Who are the people around your children? Are you one of them?

When children are younger, they spend a lot of time with their parents. This period is the perfect opportunity for us to make a lasting impact of our values on them.

When they are younger, they need parents who are firm and not pushovers, parents who are principled, who lead by example and who lay down consequences for actions.

Also, younger children need parents who enforce clear boundaries, parents who can love, show affection and are not afraid to show weaknesses as this helps to raise well-rounded children, who wouldn't grow up afraid to show their own weaknesses or emotions.

As children grow older, their needs change.

- They get tired of being told what to do.
- They want more independence.
- They want to make their own decisions and take on some responsibility.
- They want their opinions to matter.
- They want to be heard.

If they are not given the flexibility to achieve this, the bold ones will begin to disobey instructions or challenge authority. But the children not bold enough, begin to make excuses or tell tales or pretend to be well behaved.

For other children who aren't like the two classes above, they simply do what they are told without pushing back. It doesn't matter if they agree with their parents or not. Parents hardly understand what they want or what makes them happy as they simply follow the parents' lead.

This third set—children who do as they are told whether they agree with Mum and Dad or not— tend to be the most loved. They give less trouble in the home. But the downside of this is that a parent may never really get to know who that child is or what he or she truly believes in until they are a bit too grown to be impacted by their parents. Also, the children may never get to know who they are as they are too busy trying to please mum and dad and could end up never maximising their potentials.

The second set—children who fear getting into trouble at home and who result to lies and pretence—remain saints at home, while they are something else away from the home. They tend to develop a double identity. And because the parents have no clue what they get up to when they are away from the home, parents have no way of helping or supporting them.

The first set—the bolder ones who become disobedient and challenge their parents' authority—are mostly the ones who get tagged, "stubborn," "difficult," and so on.

I love the first set of children who can challenge their parents enough to ensure parents up their game. If parents are attentive to this set, they will understand the children's make-up, recognise their strengths and weaknesses and know how to help or support them as they grow.

Now, apart from these three sets, there is another set. They are the meek, gentle, well-mannered, well-behaved children who do what they are told. The difference between this set and the third set who do not push back is that these children truly believe what the parents believe and do not see the need to challenge the norm and are always perfect. Their parents understand them because they think alike. They are the same people in the home and away from the home. A few parents have these types of children. Congratulations if you do, as you might just have an easier job of raising them.

Returning to the second set of children—the ones who result to lies to stay out of trouble at home—as they get older, leave home, and get the opportunity to be themselves, they are faced with peer pressure and often make wrong choices. They tend to get completely lost.

Some of them learn the hard way while others get lucky and avoid serious consequences. But they might have an easier life if they get the right support growing up.

Parents need to make the home conducive for their children, not only when they are younger, but also during the teen years as this is the period, they begin to spend more time with their peers and in some cases, prefer to spend more time with their peers than with their parents.

If the home is not conducive, the children find more reasons to stay away. In homes where parents are not flexible with their rules, with no room for negotiation or discussion, the children mostly would prefer to be away from home.

In a home where mistakes are not tolerated, the children will lie to their parents to avoid their wrath. If we always get angry when our children make mistakes and are always ready with a punishment, the children will build a defence mechanism to avoid trouble. They will become incredibly good at lying.

As a parent, have you stopped to think about why some children may prefer the company of their friends? Their friends won't reprimand or judge them or expect so much from them.

If parents instil the right discipline and values when the child is younger, before the teenage years, it makes it easier to take a more relaxed approach as they get older.

A parent's job in teaching and modelling values and behaviours starts from day one as it is easier to imbibe the right values from a younger age. Peer pressure becomes stronger during the teen years and as they begin to spend more time with friends.

Give children a safe space in the home. Let them know they can express themselves and not be judged. Also, learn to be a fun parent and play with your children. This is another reason why some children prefer to spend more time with friends than with family because they don't get enough fun at home and there is probably nobody to chat with about the stuff that interests them. Perhaps the parents are too uptight.

What if the parents were fun and they could play together and not take life too seriously?

- Wouldn't children be inclined to want to hang out with their parents?
- Wouldn't they be inclined to tell you more about their lives and what's going on in their friends' groups?
- Wouldn't they want your advice when they get a bit confused and maybe too embarrassed to ask a friend?

As parents, we have a better chance of influencing our children's choices without telling them what to do. They would be more inclined to make responsible choices after having that chat with Mum or Dad.

In a nutshell, we stand a better chance of being able to influence our teens if they are close enough to us to trust us with the details of their lives as they grow and if they believe they won't be judged or treated harshly.

If you draw your children close and they see you as their friend, there is a much better chance that they will let you in and confide in you. Otherwise, they might be going through a lot in their lives you won't know about and wouldn't be able to help with. And if you cannot help them, they will be at the mercy of those closest to them for advice and support. If those closest to them are good friends, you will be grateful. But what if they aren't?

Do not think because your child is smart, he or she cannot get lost in a maze.

Even the smartest of children get confused at some point and rely on the advice of their close friends.

It is important that as children grow, we begin to change our mindset about parent-child relations. There is still room for rules and boundaries but ensuring they understand the reason behind what they should and should not do and how it benefits them is important.

Ensuring that you understand them enough to enable you to know the areas to support them as they grow is important.

Creating the room for the right kind of communication needed at their age is also important.

Seek to deal with the challenge they face, that leads to the breaking of a home rule rather than focus on the broken rule.

Also, teach consequences of actions, not necessarily by punishment, but if something has not been done as expected then sometimes there should be a consequence so that they become more accountable for their actions.

Being a parent and not a friend during your children's teenage years puts you in the 'parent zone'. Meaning, they tell you just what they need to tell you; they tell you only what you want to hear unless they are ready for a fight.

You only know what you know out of obligation and sometimes out of strict observation. As a teenager, I lied to my parents a few times to get what I wanted or to stay out of trouble. They had no idea of some of the things I did.

The teen years is an incredibly challenging time of transitioning from childhood to adulthood and there are a lot of changes they must deal with.

It would be nice for children to have a trusted friend who has been with them all their lives, who probably understands them more than they understand themselves. A trusted friend they can rely on. A person they know has their interests at heart and is there at their side as they transition into adulthood. Don't you want to be this person to your child?

Parents should not only be there to provide protection and direction but also be that shoulder to lean on as the children grow. When the need arises, they should be there to talk to and have fun with.

We need to change our mindset if we haven't already done so and realise that what children need most, at certain times of their lives, is just a friend and nothing more. A good friend does not scold, judge, reprimand or make another feel guilty, or feel like a failure or inadequate. Can you be this friend to your children?

I have heard many parents say, "My children are my best friends." I used to say that too. But the true test of friendship I have found is this:

- Can your children tell you everything or do they hold some things back out of fear of getting blamed?
- Do they tell you just the bits you want to hear or also tell you when they messed up and made mistakes?

If they tell you just what you want to hear, without the mistakes they make, then sorry to disappoint you. You are still in the 'parent zone', which is not a bad place to be, fortunately. If you play your cards right, by the time they get past the teens, you might find yourself in the 'friend zone'.

I wouldn't say I was friends with my mum while I was a teenager, but we share such a wonderful relationship now. She must have played her cards right at some point.

Some might look back at their own teen years and see they also didn't have that 'friendship' with their parents, but they turned out okay.

While that is a fact for some, the current distractions my children must deal with are nothing compared, and they are so much more than the distractions I had to deal with when I was a teen. If I can make them better prepared or make it easier for them to navigate the world by doing more now, then I will.

Strategizing

Old habits can be a challenge for parents, but we cannot keep doing the same things repeatedly and expect a different result. If something is not working, change it and try something else.

I previously mentioned how I was a chronic yeller in my home. When my children misbehaved, they expected to hear mummy yell and reprimand them in frustration and their expectations were never cut short.

My yelling worked perfectly when they were younger because if they wanted to avoid it, they tried to do what was right. But at some point, they got used to it and I became the dog that barks but never bites.

As children become teenagers, they begin to believe that they know it all and have heard it all. Following instructions become a struggle for some.

You need to know your children. If they are the types that struggle in this area, make them feel comfortable around you so that they know you are on their side. Draw them close and quit the power struggle for a while. Make them your friends and give them friendly advice.

Teenagers and adults think differently. If this wasn't the case, raising teenagers would be a piece of cake.

Research says a teenager's brain doesn't develop fully until the mid-20s. The part of the brain matured adults use in decision making and controlling impulses, is still under development during the teen years. Parents role in guiding their children, influencing their values and behaviours is critical to their growth, how they think, and process their feelings.[v]

This shows that your teenage children still need a lot of guidance for a few years. If they struggle to follow your instructions, instead of focusing on fighting over every issue and pushing them further away, find level ground and try to give them advice from a trusted friend.

No matter how opinionated and strong-willed a child is, they will listen to advice from a friend. So, fix the relationship and then offer guidance. Apply different strategies to ensure you can get through to them, to get results.

I have a few more questions here.

- Do you have a parenting strategy, or do you just wing it, as some would say?
- Are you stuck on old habits just because that is what you know best or, that's how your parents raised you?
- If you have a strategy, does it work? Can you see the results?

- Do you have different strategies for different children?
- Does the strategy that works for child A work for child B? Or do you need to be innovative?

If you have children with different personality types and temperaments, using the same techniques for them might be challenging. If you are currently struggling with parenting, this is your cue to learn new ways, try new techniques, discover new tricks, and try something different.

I am still a recovering yeller. I have always known that yelling at my children does not equate to being a great mum, but this was something I picked up from my mum which goes to show how behaviours are transferable.

Don't get me wrong, my mum was and is still a great mum. She did a fantastic job of raising five biological children and more non-biological ones.

Funnily enough, I used to think that yelling was a common behaviour among African mums, but I have since learnt that it cuts across ethnic boundaries. It is an issue a lot of mums struggle with.

Anyway, I knew that at some point the children would get used to it like I did as a teenager, and it would make no difference to them whether I yelled or not. I also knew that I had to change, more so because the children were getting older, and I wanted to be able to communicate effectively. I did not have an option.

I started to make a conscious effort. It was a difficult journey, but I was determined. I read books, listened to parenting courses and did everything I could to stop a habit that was so deep-rooted.

At some point, I gave my children the responsibility to call me out whenever I yelled as I was determined to drop that habit. How they loved that task. I knew that if I must stop, I needed some form of accountability and who was best to call me out if not the children?

I also realised that I had to change some old techniques if I needed lasting results.

When they were younger children, I gave instructions and they obeyed. But as older children, they respond to instructions in different ways. Even when they disagree, as long as they are in my home, they have to obey. But

I prefer that they choose to obey as opposed to being compelled to obey so that when they leave my home, they wouldn't need me to tell them to do the right thing. They'll choose to do it.

With better understanding, I became intentional in ensuring everything I did with and around my children would strengthen our bond and build the trust we shared.

I developed a friendlier approach and a less authoritarian one (this was when I created the Yeller Chart, seeing how my children also began to yell at each other). I found new ways to communicate to bring myself to their level and help me understand what was going on in their world.

I became more patient and a better listener. I fought the urge to judge them or reprimand them whenever they told me something that exposed their weaknesses. This allowed me to have more 'ammunition' in my relationship with them. Every discussion became a teachable moment without necessarily dishing out instructions as I would have done previously.

When children hear something repeatedly in the right environment it sticks, even without them realising it.

I have created avenues for discussions and negotiations where we have intelligent exchanges without me expecting to have the final say all the time. This makes them feel they are being heard and gives them a sense of maturity.

I have created a better environment for them to thrive and be themselves where they can make guided choices. I also know what areas of their development to focus on and the areas not to worry about. I can trust them more because I am more aware of their thoughts and challenges.

Also, I can help them to be better individuals as we go on each day together. They are more open to discussions and express their opinions even when we do not agree. This is building a level of trust and strengthening our bond and while it is still a work in progress, I understand my children better and I know what goes on in their world mostly.

I am intentional about making out time for them, even with my busy schedule, and as a result, parenting has become less of a chore and a lot more fun. I can see positive results already in who they are becoming.

My children still have a few years on this teenage journey, but I am confident that if I continue what I have started, we will go on this journey together and they will be more confident individuals, positively contributing to society while exhibiting the right values.

Here are some of my dos and don'ts you can adopt to guide you on your journey with your children.

- Come down to their level and see things from their perspective.
- Encourage and recognise hard work and celebrate it.
- Spend time with them, bring down your guard and just play with them.
- Show interest in things they enjoy and share in their excitement.

- Create avenues for discussions and allow them to open up to you.
- Take time to establish a good relationship, by switching from parent mode to friend mode regularly.
- Ensure you know who they hang out with; know their friends.
- Choose your battles.
- Do not use their weaknesses against them; deliberately build trust.
- Do not be too rigid; negotiate with them to strike that balance.
- Do not act as though you are perfect; share life lessons and experiences.
- Do not put undue pressure on your child; learn to pull back.
- Do not be too busy to notice changes in behaviour, which could be a cry for help.
- Do not make a mountain out of a molehill; stop constant criticism and comparison.
- Do not condemn; correct them with love.

This is not an exhaustive list, so you can create your bullet points from what you have read so far or learnt elsewhere and add them to the list.

More on Parenting

Let's elaborate on some of the points in my list of dos and don'ts of parenting.

One of the points mentioned is learning to 'pull back'. How does a parent pull back?

Pulling back involves understanding what you are doing wrong and making a conscious effort to take a step back, evaluate your position as a parent, strategize and intentionally let go of some areas of control.

- Do your children like making their breakfast? Let them.
- Do they like picking their clothes? Let them.

Think of areas that can have little or no consequence if not done right and start giving them more freedom in these areas.

- Are you always in their space?
- Do you monitor every step or move they make?

Take a step back. I do not advocate completely relinquishing authority but loosen restrictions. Provide appropriate guidance in all these areas and then let them have some control over their affairs.

You can check in on them now and again and chip in some advice as they go on but give them some space. Be more flexible with some rules and soften your approach. This would allow you more time to focus on the things that matter.

The first point on my dos and don'ts list is coming down to their level. Sometimes, this is necessary. If you want to have a better understanding of what's going in that child's mind, take off your parent hat and just hang out with them, put yourself in their shoes.

Get into their world, play games with them, go for walks, have discussions, try fun activities. If you have more than one child, then create time to spend with each child separately so that they can have your full attention.

Ask questions about their friends, school, their interest and so on. Let them be themselves when they are around you.

Show interest in the things they enjoy and spend as much time with them as possible. This gives you a better understanding of what goes on in their lives. You will know your child better and if there are areas they struggle, you will be able to gradually build them up from a place of love and friendship—and not just from a parent's perspective—which would make it easier for them to listen to you.

Sometimes, suppress the urge to tell them off immediately even when they make a mistake or make a wrong judgement. Listen instead, enjoy the story, laugh with them, and then make a mental note to correct them lovingly on the topic after having a good laugh.

Do not spoil the fun by correcting them at every opportunity, particularly if it's something minor. Children have a good way of leaving out the bits about what they did wrong, in their storytelling. This happens more often when they expect to get in trouble for their behaviour. But if you make it a habit to avoid constantly picking out their errors, they'll be more relaxed to tell you about their experiences. It is better to be aware of the wrong your child does in your absence. When you are aware, you can find ways to help them improve over time. They don't always have to get told off for every wrong. This is where choosing your battles comes into play—another point on my list.

Do not let their weaknesses steal the fun when you spend time with them as these are priceless moments and an opportunity to strengthen that bond and subsequently build trust. Let your everyday lives be made up of teachable moments instead. Teach by example most importantly, so it's not a case of "do what I say and not what I do."

Do not make a mountain out of a molehill. Do not exaggerate every poor choice of behaviour or dwell on every mistake. Make a conscious effort to stop constant criticisms, no matter how challenging your child is. Try to look out for the positives and focus on them. Correct from a place of love and encouragement.

Another issue parents have is comparison, which has been touched on slightly in a previous chapter. Don't compare one child with another or with a peer. This is usually done to encourage the children to work harder but why not get them to be the best versions of themselves instead.

If there must be any comparison or competition, let them only compete with their own performance and work to beat their previous records. This way the feeling of never being enough or always wanting to please Mum and Dad wouldn't be something they struggle with.

If you are dealing with challenging children, change your strategy. Negotiate as they get older. Open avenues for discussions as stated earlier. Find out what their concerns are. Switch from parent mode to friend mode as you come down to their level as often as possible.

I cannot overemphasise the importance of knowing and understanding your children. Do not shut them down when they ask questions or challenge your authority. Instead, listen to them, allow them to ask questions, find out from them why they have their perspective and deal with the root cause and not the behaviour.

Spend more time modelling your family values than complaining about their behaviour.

Encourage them constantly and let them see the benefit of good behaviour by sharing life lessons, telling them stories and experiences.

Let them know that you too are not perfect, and this could help boost their self-confidence when they make mistakes.

Allow them to make mistakes sometimes and let them face the consequences of their mistakes. This helps them become more resilient as they learn to get back on their feet.

You might wonder about the long list of dos and don'ts. Trust me, it's easier stated than done. However, do not beat yourself up. Parenting is a learning process, and we are all a work in progress. Once we know what to do, what to work on and we keep at it, we will get positive results.

Applying just 50% of the areas addressed in this book would be doing something differently from the old techniques and this new application will yield significant results.

Sometimes we might think that we know it all and have done it all. Or we might think we have missed all the opportunities to do the right things when the time was right. But you do not know it all. You have not done it all and you still have some time to get it right if your children are still growing.

The most important aspect of parenting is covered in my next chapter "The God factor."

5

THE GOD FACTOR

This is a tricky area for anyone reading who is not a Christian parent. However, do not worry because it all comes together in the end. Still, I will ask,

What do you believe in? Are you a person of faith?

My faith as a Christian mum is a relevant part of who I am and helps to shape my values. I rely on God for direction every day and on His grace. It is important to note that God is love. The Holy Bible teaches us to love one another, and it is safe to assume that we all love our children. Irrespective of your faith, whether you believe in God or not, the values the Christian faith teaches are very much in line with good parenting, as Christianity ultimately teaches love.

The Holy Bible states that as parents we should

> *"Train up a child in the way he should go and when he is old, he will not depart from it."*[vi]

I hold on to these words. It is important for me as a child of God to ensure that I train my children aright.

God has given me the responsibility to nurture my children and I do not take it lightly. He has also given us free will and I have chosen to use my free will to serve Him, seek His direction and do His will, which includes training up my children in the way of the Lord.

Our children also have free will and at some points in their lives, they will choose to exercise that same free will and could choose not to follow the teachings they have been given by their parents. If that happens, what do we do?

We have no control over their future choices, no matter how well we train them. Although it is highly unlikely that a well brought up child would completely derail from the right path, we cannot see the future and do not know all the challenges they will encounter, as the right path has become so unclear in today's world.

It takes the grace of God to stick to the right path. The wrong paths tend to be the easier ones. As parents, we must do our best and rest assured that we have done so. We must trust God's word concerning our children and believe every word spoken about our children.

The Holy Bible states that,

> *"Behold, children are a heritage from the Lord,*
>
> *The fruit of the womb is a reward... Happy is the man who has his quiver full of them ... "*[vii]

Note the word 'Happy'. This means my children would bring me happiness and not sorrow.

Again, the Holy Bible states that,

> *"My children shall be taught of the Lord and great shall be their peace."* (Paraphrased)[viii]

This implies that my children will dwell in great peace. Understanding this verse was the end of my worries about my children. It became clear to me that no matter the mistakes I make as a parent, they will still be taught of the Lord and great shall be their peace.

There are so many dos and don'ts in parenting, but it is important to understand that you cannot control your children's choices. You can influence them as much as you can with the right directions, but you must trust that they will make the right choices once you've done your bit.

It's not enough to follow rules or follow outlined processes. If we trust God to finish what He started when He blessed us with these children and depend on Him to bless our efforts, He will give us the strength and wisdom to do it right and He will be our strength in times of weakness.

Do not beat yourself up if you did not pay attention to that child during his or her teenage years or if you feel you had been too busy to find the time to bond with your children. Just desire to raise Godly well- rounded children and make every effort you can, then leave God to bless your effort. Remember the Holy Bible states that *"He will bless the work of our hands."*[ix] So, we have to put our hands to work in raising our children to enable Him to bless our works.

I was listening to a popular television preacher recently and took note of a phrase he mentioned. He said, "don't be too focused on the how but be focused on the who."

No number of mistakes we make can change who we are in God. Yes, we might have made mistakes but that's just what we did and not who we are. This speaks for us and our children.

In my opinion, this is the most important chapter of this book. As a Christian, I understand the importance of the God factor. We can do our best as parents, but our children can grow up and still be influenced by peers or still choose to ignore their upbringing and make wrong choices, but that's where God's favour comes in.

We can make parenting mistakes or get it completely wrong but out of our weaknesses, God can choose to favour our children in ways we or they do not deserve.

Remember God doesn't want you hooked on a formula or system but hooked on Him. Therefore, if you are not a Christian and you do not believe in the power of the supernatural being, God our Father, I can only pray that you have a personal encounter with Him to understand fully what this chapter is about.

Whenever I struggle with anything, I take it to God. Yes, there are strategies and processes to follow but you can know all of these and struggle to do them or do them and struggle to see results. You can also know and do all of these and see good results, still, your children can choose to throw it all out of the window when they get older.

The only anchor that never fails, is putting every area of your life in God's hands. Seek His guidance, ask Him for solutions and constantly seek His face.

Sometimes, it is possible to be overwhelmed with the responsibility of raising children while juggling work and other commitments. I have decided to always do my best and let God do the rest as I know my best can never be enough. Once you can do this, even you will wonder how you are able to get the right balance in every area of your life.

We need to seek God always for strength, patience, and wisdom. These are three virtues that every parent needs.

Do you have a rebellious child—a child who wants to have his or her way all the time or a child going in a different direction from the family? Have you tried all you know and all you've learnt? Then turn your attention to God.

Are you having a fantastic time as a parent? Are all your children easy to manage, with no challenging behaviour? Still, fix your attention on God, constantly thanking Him for his favour as you successfully parent those children.

As a Christian parent, I choose to pray for my children every day, asking God to help me bring them up the right way; asking Him to provide all that I need to bring them up in the right environment.

If you are a Christian, it is wise to introduce your children to God and His Word. Expose them to Bible teachings from a young age and put them in God's hands. Who else will do a better job of raising your children other than the creator Himself? There is no situation God cannot change. There is no personality issue or behavioural problem that He cannot fix. So, why not put Him in charge and let him take the wheel. Be still and know that He is God!

You might be worried about your children; you might have tried your best as a parent but still cannot see results. I implore you to let go and let God. Put your trust in Him completely and let Him be the Lord of your home. He is working behind the scenes and putting things right for you and your children. Dare to trust Him completely. Let Him rule in the affairs of your home and rest assured that God has got your back.

In a nutshell, do your best in raising your children, learn and improve on your parenting skills, but most importantly, let God take the lead.

This is my belief as a Christian. Are you a Christian parent? Do you believe in the supernatural being? Your response will determine how you apply the teachings covered in this chapter.

6

SUMMARY AND CONCLUSION

We have discussed various challenges in raising teens such as behavioural challenges, poor parenting skills, parenting techniques and letting God take the wheel.

Most of the areas covered have been inspired by personal experiences from being a teen to becoming a mother. I am also learning every day because parenting is a daily and continuous classroom. No knowledge is lost and having a culture of learning helps me to improve on myself as an individual.

The burning desire to share what I have learnt on my parenting journey motivated me to write this book. My parenting journey might just have been a bit easier if I

SUMMARY AND CONCLUSION

read a book like this on parenting in the early years of my journey. However, the challenges and strategies covered in this book are not exhaustive.

Once you have read through this book, take some time to think and reflect on your circumstances.

If you have teenagers who are strong-willed and you find yourself always in a power struggle and they don't listen, or, if you think you do not have the right relationship with your teenagers and you want to make it better, then consider applying some of the techniques mentioned in this book. Take one step at a time.

I recommend starting with yourself. Work on your well-being, ensure you are well placed to focus on the strategies mentioned. Once you begin to see results, do not relent. Continue with the process and when you find that you stumble and fall back to bad habits, don't beat yourself up, instead pick yourself up and carry on.

The first signs of change can be very satisfying, and you might think for once that you know what you're doing as a parent but then the results you see and how long it takes depends a lot on how well you know your child and what strategy you have chosen. Once your strategy works, you can repeat the process.

By repeat, I do not only mean repeating the specific thing you did that worked but repeating the whole journey; not just your specific actions.

Continue to be intentional, continue striving to understand your children as they evolve, continue learning new ways to interact with them and engage, apply new strategies if required in line with their age, personalities and circumstances and just keep learning.

Most importantly keep relying on God. Keep doing the things you have learnt and keep getting better at them.

Lastly, keep loving your children as love is a powerful tool.

I hope you have learnt a thing or two reading through the chapters of this book.

Remember there is no rule book on parenting as every child is different and not one rule fits all. It is your responsibility to find what works for you and your children.

Today's children are tomorrow's leaders; they will make up the future of society. We need to build a society with the right values and the best way to ensure this is to instil these values in our children today. This should be our priority.

What good will it be to focus all our time on amassing wealth or achieving great accomplishments if we fail to raise the children who will carry on after us?

Let your children be your priority and the focus in your home. They will grow up quickly and soon, you will have all your time to yourself. Then you can choose to do whatever it is that stops you from spending valuable time with them today. Choose wisely how you spend your time now.

ACKNOWLEDGEMENTS

I want to express my gratitude to God who is my ever-present help.

To my husband, Clement Awenlimobor, for continually being my rock and for standing by me. And to my beloved children who have been my inspiration.

I also want to acknowledge Ola Olaleye, who wrote the foreword to this book; Florence Igboayaka, who helped bring my idea to life; my beloved parents and siblings who have always been a huge support.

Lastly, a heartfelt appreciation to everyone who contributed in some way to make this book a reality and to those who took out time to read, offer feedback and write their reviews.

EndNotes

[i] How Social Learning Theory Works by Kendra Cherry. www.verywellmind.com
[ii] https://dictionary.cambridge.org/dictionary/english/values
[iii] Proverbs 22 verse 6. (King James Bible)
[iv] These dates are based on a study by Pew Research Centre, updated in 2019. www.pewresearch.org
[v] Brain Development in Pre-teens and Teenagers. www.raisingchildren.net.au
[vi] Proverbs 22 verse 6 (King James Bible)
[vii] Psalm 127 verse 3 and 5 (New King James Version)
[viii] Isaiah 54 verse 13 (New King James Version)
[ix] Deuteronomy 28 verse 12 (New King James Version)

Printed in Great Britain
by Amazon